Native Americans

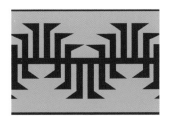

Yurok

Barbara A. Gray-Kanatiiosh

ABDO Publishing Company

visit us at
www.abdopublishing.com

Published by ABDO Publishing Company, 4940 Viking Drive, Edina, Minnesota 55435. Copyright © 2007 by Abdo Consulting Group, Inc. International copyrights reserved in all countries. No part of this book may be reproduced in any form without written permission from the publisher. The Checkerboard Library™ is a trademark and logo of ABDO Publishing Company.

Printed in the United States.

Cover Photo: Marilyn "Angel" Wynn/Nativestock.com
Interior Photos: AP/WideWorld p. 29; Corbis pp. 4, 30
Illustrations: David Kanietakeron Fadden pp. 7, 9, 11, 13, 15, 17, 19, 21, 23, 25, 27
Editors: Rochelle Baltzer, Megan M. Gunderson
Art Direction & Maps: Neil Klinepier

Library of Congress Cataloging-in-Publication Data

Gray-Kanatiiosh, Barbara A., 1963-
  Yurok / Barbara A. Gray-Kanatiiosh.
    p. cm. -- (Native Americans)
  Includes bibliographical references and index.
  ISBN-10 1-59197-658-8
  ISBN-13 978-1-59197-658-5
  1. Yurok Indians--History--Juvenile literature. 2. Yurok Indians--Social life and customs--Juvenile literature.
  I. Title. II. Series: Native Americans (Edina, Minn.)

E99.Y97G7 2006
979.4004'973--dc22

2004047719

About the Author: Barbara A. Gray-Kanatiiosh, JD

Barbara Gray-Kanatiiosh, JD, Ph.D. ABD, is an Akwesasne Mohawk. She resides at the Mohawk Nation and is of the Wolf Clan. She has a Juris Doctorate from Arizona State University, where she was one of the first recipients of ASU's special certificate in Indian Law. Barbara's Ph.D. is in Justice Studies at ASU. She is currently working on her dissertation, which concerns the impacts of environmental injustice on indigenous culture. Barbara works hard to educate children about Native Americans through her writing and Web site, where children may ask questions and receive a written response about the Haudenosaunee culture. The Web site is: www.peace4turtleisland.org

About the Illustrator: David Kanietakeron Fadden

David Kanietakeron Fadden is a member of the Akwesasne Mohawk Wolf Clan. His work has appeared in publications such as *Akwesasne Notes*, *Indian Time*, and the *Northeast Indian Quarterly*. Examples of his work have also appeared in various publications of the Six Nations Indian Museum in Onchiota, NY. His work has also appeared in "How the West Was Lost: Always the Enemy," produced by Gannett Production, which appeared on the Discovery Channel. David's work has been exhibited in Albany, NY; the Lake Placid Center for the Arts; Centre Strathearn in Montreal, Quebec; North Country Community College in Saranac Lake, NY; Paul Smith's College in Paul Smiths, NY; and at the Unison Arts & Learning Center in New Paltz, NY.

Contents

Where They Lived

The Yurok (YOO-ruhk) call themselves *Olekwo'l*, which means "persons." Many Native Americans use this term to refer to themselves. The Yurok **dialect** is part of the Algonquian language family. Some Yurok also spoke the language of their closest neighboring tribe.

The name *Yurok* is a Karok word that means "downstream." The word describes the location of the Yurok in relation to the Karok along the Klamath River. Tolowa, Hupa, and Wiyot tribes also lived near the Yurok.

Yurok homelands were located in present-day California, from Trinidad to Crescent City. Some Yurok lived in villages along the Pacific Ocean. Beaches, lagoons, and salt marshes were common landforms in this region. Seals and sea lions often played near the ocean.

Some Yurok occupied coastal lands like this cove in northern California.

4

Other Yurok set up inland villages near the lower part of the Klamath River. This area contained rivers, streams, and grasslands. Thick forests of redwood, pine, and oak trees also filled parts of the inland areas. Deer, elk, and rabbits lived in the forested lands.

Yurok Homelands

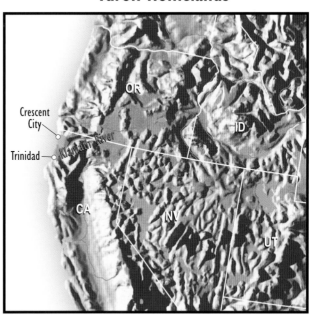

Society

Yurok society had little political organization and no chiefs. However, in each village a wealthy man called a *peyerk* acted as leader. Elders were responsible for training a man to become a peyerk. During training, the soon-to-be peyerk went on a vision quest. At this sacred time, he communicated with nature and the spirit world.

Sometimes, peyerk from each village met to resolve arguments among the tribe. Peyerk also hosted tribal ceremonies. At these times, they supplied food and shelter for the Yurok. They also provided special clothing for the dancers.

Peyerk lived in homes at higher elevations than other Yurok. They also wore finer clothing. And, they spoke in a more elaborate style. Occasionally, peyerk spoke in foreign languages.

Yurok medicine people were called shamans. Shamans were usually women. A young woman became a shaman after dreaming of being told to do so. Then, another shaman assisted her in a **ritual** dance. Shamans used plants, prayers, and rituals to heal people. They also performed ceremonies to ensure successful hunting, fishing, and gathering.

Each year, the Yurok came together for the World Renewal Ceremony. At these times, the tribe performed ceremonial songs and dances that had been passed on for many generations. Dancers wore elaborate clothing for the occasion.

At times, peyerk provided clothing for as many as 13 dancers. Some peyerk inherited ceremonial clothing and ornaments.

Food

The Yurok ate a variety of foods found in their environment. To obtain their food, they hunted, fished, and gathered. The tribe hunted seals, sea lions, elk, and deer. They used spears, traps, and bows and arrows to hunt these large animals. The Yurok also hunted rabbits, ducks, and geese. They caught these smaller animals with traps, snares, and nets.

The Yurok fished for sturgeons, eels, and salmon in the ocean or in the rivers. They used woven traps, nets, and hooks and lines to catch them. Then the women baked, broiled, or sun dried the fish.

Along the coast, the Yurok gathered clams, mussels, and other shellfish. Sometimes, they ate whales that became stranded in shallow waters. Inland, the Yurok gathered berries, wild plants, seed, and acorns.

Acorns were a basic source of food for the tribe. The Yurok stored them in woven willow granaries. These tight fitted granaries prevented insects and animals from eating the acorns.

To prepare acorns for eating, Yurok women ground them into flour using a **mortar** and **pestle**. Then, they leached the flour to remove poisonous **tannic acid**. This involved pouring hot water over the flour several times to wash out the acid. Finally, the women boiled the flour with water to make mush. They also made soup and bread with acorn flour.

Yurok men often used woven nets to catch fish. They also made weirs. A weir is a type of enclosure that is set into water to trap fish.

Homes

While traveling, the Yurok lived in temporary brush shelters. But throughout most of the year, they lived in rectangular plank houses built from redwood. These homes were sturdy and lasted for many years. They were passed on from generation to generation and named to reflect the owners.

There were many steps to building a plank home. First, the men cut planks from redwood trees. They were able to do this without killing the trees. Then, they used stone tools to split, carve, and shape the wood.

The Yurok built each home above a deep pit. They covered the inside of the pit with the redwood planks. To construct the frame, they used redwood logs and cross poles. They left a hole in the roof for light to enter and smoke to exit. And, in the right-hand corner there was an entry hole that was two feet (.5 m) wide.

Yurok men used smaller plank houses as sweat houses. Sweating was a way to purify oneself. So, the Yurok believed that spending time in sweat houses strengthened one's spiritual and physical health.

Sweat houses were built over a pit containing rocks and a fire. The men heated the rocks and poured water over them to make steam. They held ceremonies, worked on tools, and exchanged gossip in the sweat houses.

Plank homes provided protection from cold, wet winters. They also offered storage space for personal items. The Yurok lined the interior walls with storage baskets, household items, and hunting and fishing tools.

Clothing

The Yurok used natural items found in their environment to make clothing. Before European influence, they wore clothing made from plants and animals.

The men wore **breechcloths** made from rabbit skins or deer hides. Sometimes, a man wore a type of net fabric around his waist. He carried items in this netting, which was made from rolled feathers and plant fibers.

Yurok women usually wore aprons made from rabbit skins or deer hides. But sometimes, they made aprons from strips of inner tree bark. Women often wore capes made from animal hides or furs. They also received **tattoos**.

Both men and women wore deer-hide moccasins. The bottoms of the moccasins were made from elk hides. This protected their feet from rocks and thorns. And on cold days, the Yurok wore robes made from deer, coyote, or raccoon furs.

Men and women also wore necklaces made from bones, stones, wooden beads, and shells. The Yurok used a certain type of shell as currency. They made purses from elk antlers to carry these shells.

The Yurok decorated their clothing with shells and juniper berries. On special occasions, men wore ceremonial headbands made from red-headed woodpecker scalps.

13

Crafts

The Yurok used twined baskets for daily tasks, such as gathering and cooking foods. The women used hazel, willow, and conifer roots to make the baskets. And they used squaw grass, maidenhair fern, woodwardia fern, and porcupine quills to create designs on them.

Yurok women made large baskets for gathering acorns and firewood. These baskets had woven straps that allowed the women to carry them on their backs. The straps fit around the basket and across the forehead.

The women made several types of cooking baskets. A hopper basket was bowl shaped and had a large hole at the bottom. When the women ground seed and nuts, they placed a hopper basket over a **mortar**. This kept the seed and nut **meal** from falling onto the ground. Then, they used a sifting basket to clean the meal. Finally, they cooked the meal inside a boiling basket.

Yurok women also wove fancy basket hats. They decorated them with beautiful designs. A Yurok woman wore one hat for everyday use and another for special occasions. Widows wore different hats that symbolized their loss.

Twining was a common Yurok basket making style. To do this, the women set the materials in rows. Then, they wove in and out of the rows in one direction.

Family

Yurok families and villages owned certain parts of land for hunting, fishing, and gathering. Throughout the year, they traveled to those areas to obtain food. They gathered items such as water lily seed, redwood, and acorns in those areas.

Women were in charge of several important tasks for their family and village. They cooked, wove baskets, and looked after the children.

The women also made clothing. To do this, they scraped away extra meat from animal hides. Then, they **tanned** the hides to make them soft. Next, the women stretched them out to dry in the sun. And finally, they sewed the hides into a piece of clothing.

Men were responsible for other necessary tasks. They made cooking tools such as stone **mortars**, **pestles**, and bowls. The men also carved spoons from wood or elk horns. To carve these tools, they used sharp knives made from **obsidian**.

The men also made hunting and fishing tools. They wove twined fish traps. And, they built wooden weirs. When fish were caught in these traps, the men used nets to scoop them out.

Yurok men were in charge of carving tools.

Children

Yurok children learned much from elders. In Yurok society, the elders were important keepers of knowledge. They often told stories to the children to help them learn about Yurok **culture** and history. Elders also taught children traditional songs and dances.

Children learned everyday tasks by watching and helping the adults. The women taught the girls how to make baskets. Girls learned where to gather basket materials and how to prepare them for weaving. This included learning how to dig for conifer roots and split them. And, the women showed them how to use plants to dye the baskets.

Boys learned how to make hunting and fishing tools. The men taught them how to make animal traps. Boys also learned how to make **obsidian** knives. To do this, they used a deer horn to chip and shape the obsidian.

Still, the children had plenty of time to play. Double ball was one of their favorite games. It was played by three teams of three. Players carried wooden bats that were 35 inches (89 cm) long.

The double ball was made from two bottle-shaped pieces of carved wood. Each piece was about five inches (13 cm) long. The two pieces were attached by two inches (5 cm) of twine.

The object of the game was to get the double ball into another team's goal area. Teammates threw the ball to each other and caught it with the bat.

Double ball was a common game that the Yurok played. Villages often competed against each other.

Myths

The Yurok pass on many types of myths, or stories. This helps younger generations understand Yurok **culture** and history. The following is one myth about how salmon came to the Yurok.

Long ago, Trickster became hungry. Mink told him that Grandma Salmon kept fish in a pond behind her home. "I shall go to visit her," Trickster said. Trickster's nephew gave him some red berries for the journey.

Trickster arrived at Grandma Salmon's home and knocked on the door. "Come in. You look hungry. Would you like some acorn mush?" she asked. Trickster popped some red berries in his mouth and offered some to Grandma. But Grandma thought the berries were salmon eggs. She was shocked! "How does he know about the salmon in my pond?" Grandma wondered.

"I cannot feed him mush. He wants fish," Grandma thought. So, she took her net to the pond and scooped out a large salmon. She cooked it and fed Trickster. Then, Trickster played his flute, and Grandma fell asleep to the beautiful music. The magical flute began to play by itself.

While the flute played, Trickster snuck out to the pond. He dug a path from the pond to the river so the fish could be freed.

But, Grandma awoke with a feeling that something was wrong. "No one can play the flute that long," she thought. Just then, she saw Trickster lift the last shovelful of soil that separated the pond from the river. The salmon had been freed.

According to Yurok myth, Trickster set salmon free into the river.

War

The Yurok were peaceful people who maintained good relations with their neighbors. Their society depended on trading with nearby tribes. The Yurok often traded acorns, fish, shells, beads, baskets, hides, **obsidian**, and bows with their neighbors.

But when necessary, the Yurok fought to protect their people and lands. Prior to fighting, they held a war dance. During battle, the warriors wore body armor to protect themselves. One type of armor was made of thick elk hide. Yurok warriors used bone or obsidian knives as weapons.

The Yurok also defended themselves with wooden bows and arrows. They wrapped their bows with **sinew** to make them stronger. They also used sinew to make the bow strings. The average Yurok bow was about four feet (1 m) long. Warriors carved the arrows from wood. Then, they used sinew to attach obsidian arrowheads to the arrows.

The Yurok often used dugout canoes to flee to safety. They also used the canoes to transport trade goods. Men made paddles and dugout canoes from redwood. They used stone tools to carve and shape the wood.

Yurok warriors were brave and strong.

Contact with Europeans

The Yurok first came into contact with Europeans in 1775. Spanish explorer Juan Francisco de la Bodega met the tribe while spending several days in Trinidad Bay. Eventually, the Yurok and the Europeans began trading goods.

In 1848, gold was discovered in California. Soon, miners and settlers flooded California. Around 1850, a seaport was built in Yurok territory. This made travel to goldfields more convenient for the newcomers. However, **culture** clashes arose as new communities formed in Yurok territory. The Yurok were forced to take the lowest-paying jobs.

Soon, mounting conflicts led to violence. So in 1855, a rule was made to disarm Native Americans. And, anyone who sold firearms to a Native American would be punished. Some people resisted, leading to a brief war. Later that year, the Klamath River **Reservation** was established.

Then in 1864, the Hoopa Valley Reservation was established. And in 1891, it combined with the Klamath River Reservation to form the Yurok Reservation.

The Yurok **Reservation** started with 58,168 acres (23,540 ha) of land. But after land sales, the reservation was reduced to about 6,800 acres (2,800 ha). Three plots of land became the **rancherias** of Big Lagoon, Trinidad, and Resighini.

Traders were some of the first Europeans to come into contact with the Yurok. Both the Yurok and the Europeans had items that were valuable to each other.

Lucy Thompson

Yurok leaders have worked hard to protect the tribe. This includes supporting hunting and fishing rights, as well as history and **cultural** traditions.

Lucy Thompson was a leader in preserving Yurok history and culture. She was born in 1856. Thompson was a Klamath River Yurok. Her Yurok name was *Che-ne-wah Weitch-ah-wah*. She was a wealthy woman in her tribe.

In 1916, Thompson wrote an autobiography titled *To the American Indian: Reminiscences of a Yurok Woman*. She wrote the book at a time when Yurok culture was threatened.

Thompson felt that **anthropologists** and the **media** were not writing the truth about her people. She hoped her book would provide realistic information about the Yurok. Even today, Thompson's book helps readers understand how the tribe lived during the early 1900s.

An autobiography is the story of a person's life that is written by that person. In 1992, Thompson's autobiography won an American Book Award.

The Yurok Today

In the 1970s, there was a **revival** of traditional Native American ceremonialism. At this time, elderly peyerk met to perform ceremonial dances. This helped to connect the Native American tribes in northwestern California. Today, ceremonies remain an important aspect of Yurok lifestyle and **culture**.

The Yurok are committed to protecting their language and culture. They teach Yurok children traditional stories and tribal history. They hope that this knowledge will be passed on to future generations.

The Yurok have continued to work for land rights. In 1988, they took a case to the U.S. Supreme Court. The government wanted to build roads on sites that were sacred to the Yurok and other Native Americans. However, the Yurok lost the case when the government refused to protect the lands.

As of 2000, there were about 5,800 Yurok. Today, many live on **rancherias** and **reservations**. These include Smith River Rancheria, Elk Valley Rancheria, Big Lagoon Rancheria, Resighini Rancheria, Trinidad Rancheria, and Yurok Reservation. These areas are **federally recognized**.

Today, the Yurok Tribe offers job training, language classes, and children's programs. The tribe also has a program to manage its forest resources. Following long-standing Yurok beliefs, the program aims to use resources with respect to the environment.

Today, the Yurok continue to observe ceremonies. Ty Allen is a Yurok-Karok Indian. In 2004, he participated in a ceremony for the return of sacred land to the Wiyot tribe.

29

Yurok Butch Marks carries his freshly caught salmon on the California coast. Salmon have always been sacred to his tribe.

This Yurok man rides a horse during a festival. He is dressed in traditional ceremonial clothing.

Glossary

anthropologist - a person who studies the origin, nature, and destiny of human beings.

breechcloth - a piece of hide or cloth, usually worn by men, that wraps between the legs and ties with a belt around the waist.

culture - the customs, arts, and tools of a nation or people at a certain time.

dialect - a form of a language spoken in a certain area or by certain people.

federal recognition - the U.S. government's recognition of a tribe as being an independent nation. The tribe is then eligible for special funding and for protection of its reservation lands.

meal - coarsely ground seed.

media - the medium of communication that includes television, radio, and newspapers.

mortar - a strong bowl or cup in which a material is pounded.

obsidian - a hard, glassy rock formed when lava cools.

pestle - a club-shaped tool used to pound or crush a substance.

rancheria - a semipermanent Native American village in the southwest United States, especially California.

reservation - a piece of land set aside by the government for Native Americans to live on.

revival - the state of being woken up or brought back to life.

ritual - a form or order to a ceremony.

sinew - a band of tough fibers that joins a muscle to a bone.

tan - to make a hide into leather by soaking it in a special liquid.

tannic acid - related to tannin, a bitter-tasting yellow or brown mix of chemicals.

tattoo - a permanent design made on the skin.

Web Sites

To learn more about the Yurok, visit ABDO Publishing Company on the World Wide Web at **www.abdopublishing.com**. Web sites about the Yurok are featured on our Book Links page. These links are routinely monitored and updated to provide the most current information available.

Index